GUNSTOCK CARVING:
POWER TECHNIQUES

JOSE VALENCIA

Schiffer Publishing Ltd

4880 Lower Valley Road · Atglen, PA · 19310

Schiffer Books are available at special discounts for bulk purchases for sales promotions or premiums. Special editions, including personalized covers, corporate imprints, and excerpts can be created in large quantities for special needs. For more information contact the publisher:

Published by Schiffer Publishing Ltd.
4880 Lower Valley Road
Atglen, PA 19310
Phone: (610) 593-1777; Fax: (610) 593-2002
E-mail: Info@schifferbooks.com

For the largest selection of fine reference books on this and related subjects, please visit our web site at **www.schifferbooks.com**
We are always looking for people to write books on new and related subjects. If you have an idea for a book please contact us at the above address.

This book may be purchased from the publisher.
Include $5.00 for shipping.
Please try your bookstore first.
You may write for a free catalog.

In Europe, Schiffer books are distributed by
Bushwood Books
6 Marksbury Ave.
Kew Gardens
Surrey TW9 4JF England
Phone: 44 (0) 20 8392 8585; Fax: 44 (0) 20 8392 9876
E-mail: info@bushwoodbooks.co.uk
Website: www.bushwoodbooks.co.uk

Library of Congress Control Number: 2009928942

Designed by RoS
Type set in Biondi/Zurich BT

ISBN: 978 0 7643 3370 5
Printed in China

CONTENTS

DEDICATION

This book is dedicated to my lovely and patient wife, Marina, whose support has allowed me to pursue my goals.

To my daughter, Leticia, whose humor is wittier than mine and who always keeps me in constant check.

And finally, to my son, Jose Jr., who makes me proud by wearing the uniform of the United States Army.

ACKNOWLEDGMENTS

I would like to express my deepest appreciation to Dr. Lew Jensen, whose Inspiration, Encouragement and Friendship have allowed me to change careers and make my life now my living.

Thanks go to my friend Manny Chee, owner of Don's Sport Shop in Scottsdale, AZ for providing me with his personal shotgun to be used as a canvas for my work.

Thanks to Mr. Gene McKellips, owner of Village Arms in Gap, PA for facilitating the shipping of the rifle and shotgun to his shop so that I can have them available for the photo shoot.

The basketweave pattern in this book is courtesy of James Birt Engraving Studio in Phoenix, AZ.

FOREWORD

Dear Readers:

I have enjoyed my many relationships with some of the most talented people in the world of wonderful things that can only be described as fine art.

Jose Valencia is a master of his skill in our circle, and one of the best. I have known him from the beginning of his interest in this type of work and the amazing thing is that he just keeps coming up with more and more ideas and, somehow, his work keeps improving as well. I know that many people ask him how he does it, especially in the middle of a busy lifestyle. He has also managed to produce this book – sharing some of his hard-earned skills. This is his first volume, but trust me, it won't be his last.

I think it is most amazing that on top of his personal productivity, he finds the time (and is willing) to share what he has learned. I know that he is generous to a fault, but that is just how Jose has been as a friend and a valuable contributor to our circle of talented people that we call The Inspiration & Encouragement Network.com. You must know that not every master of some exotic hand-produced skill is willing to share what has taken him or her so much time, energy, and effort to acquire. You will find that Jose is also one of our best and most capable teachers at his home/studio in Phoenix, Arizona.

I believe that finely made and hand-produced works are now a dying art. It should not be – but it is a fact – and for two reasons.

First, there are more and more amazing machines being designed that can "out produce economically" any human being on earth. And there is significantly more capacity coming from the world of intelligent machines. We need these machines and they will change the world for the better – but what of a Jose Valencia, who has also made such a huge investment in his skills? What of him, if he wishes to make a living with his artistic abilities too? I have found that there are almost magical elements in human hand investment – a deep investment of the soul – that no machine can duplicate. And even if it is left up to the I&E Network alone to see that handmade artwork survives, *trust me – handmade fine art will survive*. Jose Valencia is an important trustee now of the future of human handmade treasures.

Secondly, there is the incredible effort (both in patience and practice) that the mastery of anything requires. Anyone who goes to these lengths gains the gift of true passion for their work, but few there are that find that gift.

Jose has not only mastered some of his abilities (as you will see), but this singular quest has now become his whole life. You will find yourself inspired and encouraged, and you will meet a very gifted and capable person who has produced this book with his head, his heart, his hands and a piece of his soul. I know of all the effort it has taken to climb this mountain of success and you will learn from him, I promise.

Enjoy – and then give it a try for yourself. There is something valuable here for you too.

I count Jose as one of my most choice friends. He is truly an amazing person.

— Dr. Lew Jensen
The founder of our talented circle of
Inspiration & Encouragement People,
some very dedicated souls the world over

INTRODUCTION

My goal in this book is to share with you the knowledge that I have acquired using the high speed drill. The photos and captions will guide you through an easy to understand pictorial progression as I am doing the actual carving on the gunstocks.

Hopefully, I will inspire an interest in you in this area of power carving.

When I first began carving, I had a difficult time getting started. Good patterns, instructions, and support where hard to come by. I bought countless books on the art of metal engraving. They were a great source of inspiration and I was able to get ideas to create my own patterns.

I only found three books on gun carving. I realized there was not enough information on this subject, especially on using the new carving tools available today such as the high speed drill.

As life evolves, so do woodcarving methods and tools. Woodcarving was once done using chisels, gauges, and knives; now you can find advanced tools. Today carvings could also be done using pneumatic or electric power tools, or a combination of all of these technologies, both old and new.

I am using a pneumatic High Speed Drill that rotates at 500,000 rpm's. It is the Power Pen™ from Paragrave and it uses 1/16" burs. The Power Pen handles like a felt tip pen, and it cuts through wood like a warm knife through butter. Due to the high speed of the drill, there is no torque, no vibration, and no fatigue, so I always have total control of the Power Pen.

Incidentally, this High Speed Drill was invented by a dentist, Dr. Lew Jensen.

Dr. Lew is also the founder of Profitable Hobbies, where I get most of my carving supplies. I have at my disposal a variety of dental burs that I use to get the fine details in my carvings.

When I find a pattern that I want to carve, I cut it, copy it on a special Mylar paper, place it on the stock, and begin tracing. I use tracing paper because I am not much of an artist.

The closest experience I have to drawing is two years of general drafting in high school.

When I started carving leaves, I would sometimes miss the pattern by as much as 1/8".

It was not that critical on leaves, but as you carve scrolls, if you veer off the pattern and then come back to correct it, you create what is called "elbows".

After several weeks of carving scrolls and ending up with what looked like the stone wheels of Fred Flinstone's car, I decided to call for help.

I called a couple that lived in Las Vegas and was doing woodcarving at that time, and I asked them, "How do you do scrolls?" Their reply was, "You don't, they are too hard to do. Carve wildlife instead!"

I continued to work on my leaves, then I started to carve wildlife, but I was not satisfied with the results.

I decided to take a gunstock carving class given by Mr. Keith Hone in Benjamin, Utah.

The techniques that I learned on that three day class were just unbelievable.

I didn't know what I didn't know! My learning curve just shot straight up!

I carved an elk in that class, which I entered at the Arizona State Fair in 2004, earning a First Place Blue Ribbon. I realized it was money well spent on that carving class.

I kept carving wildlife patterns, leaves, and I also created my own version of the basketweave pattern. Although my quality of work kept getting better, I kept coming back to scrolls.

And then it hit me. If scrolls were too hard to do, nobody else is doing them!

So I kept on trying and eventually I was able to master the scroll carvings.

Now, I hope to be able to share the things that it took me a couple of years to learn so that you can shave off some time from your learning curve.

If you feel you might learn better in a classroom environment and by having hands on experience, please call my studio and enroll in a carving class. You too will be amazed at the things you will discover.

I am going to show you how to carve the scrolls and a deer pattern using the stock and forearm of a Winchester 30-30 lever action rifle. The basket weave and maple leaves pattern will be carved on a Huglu CZ-USA 28 gauge double barrel shotgun.

If you do not feel comfortable carving your own rifle or shotgun at this point, get yourself a scrap piece of wood and do the carvings there first.

It is better to ruin a dollar piece of scrap wood than to have to replace a gunstock.

As your confidence and skills grow, you can try carving on the actual gunstocks.

One thing I did when I started carving was to go to gun shows and buy used rifle stocks. Some of them were cracked, missing a piece, scratched, or just plain broken. I would clean them up, sand them off, and use the best side to practice my carvings.

I got to practice on an actual stock! Once I was pleased with the results, that carved stock became one of my samples.

Well, I guess it's time to go have some fun now and carve some awesome samples!

CARVING GUNSTOCKS

This is a Winchester 94 lever action 30-30 caliber gunstock and we will decorate it with a Western motif with scrolls. On the presentation side, we will use scrolls and a whitetail deer. Shown here are the stock and the forearm.

The patterns are transferred onto Chartpak® Mylar paper using a laser printer. Once I have the artwork on the Mylar paper, I cut the paper so it may be placed on the area I will be working on. The Mylar paper has a separate background and the Mylar itself is self-adhesive.

Make sure the artwork is centered evenly at both ends. I use a piece of paper to measure the distance. If you don't like the positioning of the stencil, it may be lifted up and reapplied.

The stencil is in place.

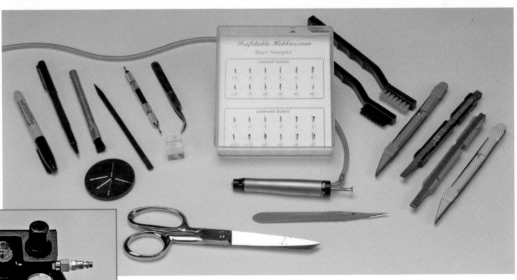

Here are all the tools needed to complete the projects. A couple of nylon brushes, a magnet to hold the burrs, sand sticks in different grits, the high speed hand piece, a nylon stick, a pin vice to hold drill bits, pens, scissors, tweezers, twelve carbide bits, and twelve diamond burrs in one case. We will not use all of these bits. We also recommend the use of a dust mask as you carve, considering all the fine dust particles thrown up.

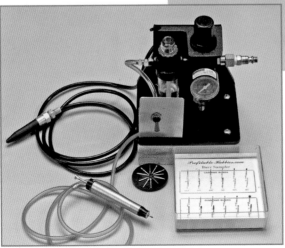

This is the Genesis System by Profitable Hobbies. I usually run my Power Pen with the regulator set at 40 psi.

RIFLE CARVING SCROLLS AND *WILDLIFE*

Full-size Patterns may be found on pgs. 51, 52 & 54

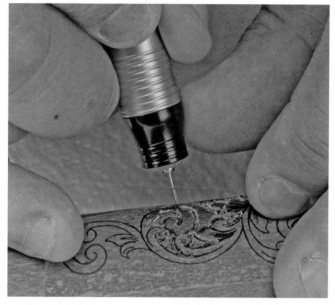

Insert a carbide bit #699 into the hand piece. Start cutting the outside line. The initial cuts for the rounding are cut at a 90-degree angle. Notice I hold and guide the bit with two fingers, making a more precise cut, as the hand piece is more stable. When working on scrolls, always remember to cut on the outside of the lines. If you cut on the inside, you may take away too much and your scrolls will be too thin. Work slowly and steadily and the scrolls will develop as they should.

In this area of the scrolls be very careful because you want to keep it round and concentric. Go in a little bit, pull the bit out and start on the outside line on the other side.

On this part of the pattern, I'm starting in the center and pulling toward me along the outside line.

Stay on the outside line and round it off, going around it.

On the tendrils, start from the center and work your way outward around the outer edge.

The pattern has been outlined.

Now we will inscribe the leaves and the tendrils using a #7611 carbide bit. This is an angled cut that will scratch the surface, outlining the leaves and tendrils along the insides.

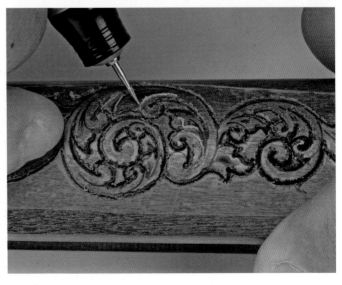

Cutting along the insides of the leaves and tendrils.

This outlines and defines where the insides of the leaves and tendrils will be.

The outlines are complete.

Use a nylon stick or a blade to lift the stencil away. First the stencil outside comes loose, and then the inside portions of the stencil are removed. This gets messy. Make sure you are very careful if you are using a blade instead of the nylon stick, as you don't want to do any unintentional carving.

Use a nylon brush now to remove any loose debris.

Using a #6 carbide bit, separate the artwork from the rest of the wood around the outline. Either a #6 or a #8 carbide bit will work for this. All this time we are only going to about 1/32" to 1/16" deep, about half the size of the little carbide ball.

Be very careful not to touch the scrolls as you outline. As you finish one side of the outlining, flip the forearm around and continue on the other side.

The outline is completed. Using the same bit, take the large parts of the negative space out, making sure not to touch the leaves, scrolls, or tendrils. The areas we will cut are marked with a Sharpie™. I recommend this exercise as a useful guide.

Using a #4 or #6 carbide, take out all the areas you have marked, being careful not to go too wide on your cuts. Eventually you will switch to a #2 carbide to take out the smaller areas of negative space.

Change to a #2 carbide now to take out the small areas you couldn't reach with the #4 or #6.

In this tight area, first cut at the outer edge of the area to be removed and work your way inward.

Now brush off the carving to remove loose debris.

Comparing the original artwork with the carving so far.

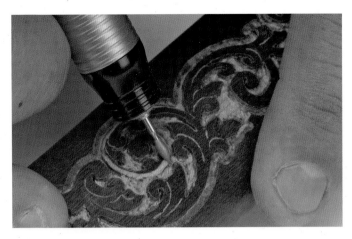

Now switch to a large diamond football and begin sculpting. Take the bit at a 45-degree angle and touch the outside. This begins rounding the carving off.

Turn the piece around to go with the flow of the scroll.

Working in this area is trickiest, rounding back the inside of the curve and making it concave.

This area is done and I'm moving on to the next portion, continuing to make it concave.

Now start taking the rest of the material lightly off the top to obtain the same color. Take off material from the top, but limit the removal to a shallow depth.

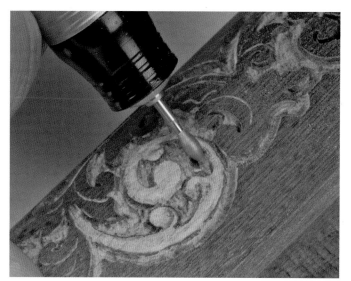

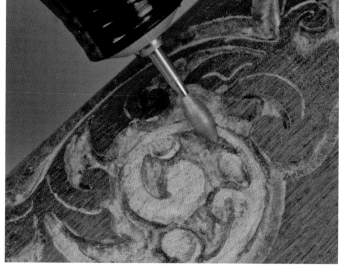

For this leaf, get behind the scroll, press down, and create a little indentation there.

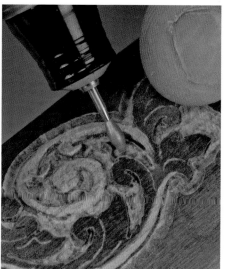

On the leaf behind the scroll, press down to separate it.

Here is the end result.

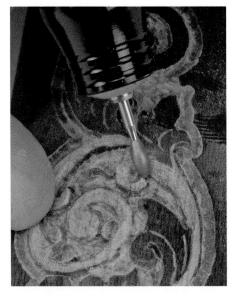
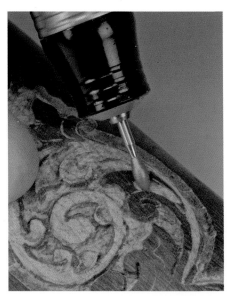

Moving to the scroll, scoop it out in the middle a little bit.

Continue scooping out leaves behind the scrolls.

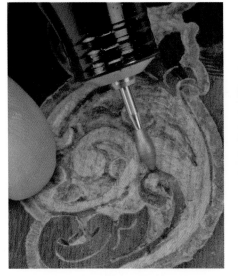

As before, move from leaf to scroll, scooping out the scroll and rounding it off. Don't worry about this rough line right now, we'll go back and clean it up later.

Scooping and separating the next leaf from the scroll.

Always try to work on the leaves behind the scrolls.

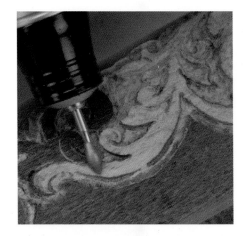

Starting on the next long scroll, take care of the outside edge first at a 45-degree angle. Don't worry about the outside line for now.

Continue sculpting the scroll lines. Working on a small scroll. The steps are the same. Begin by rounding off the outer edge as before. After it has been rounding off from both sides, lightly remove the material from the top.

Repeat these steps with the next stroll at the outer end.

Scooping out the last scroll.

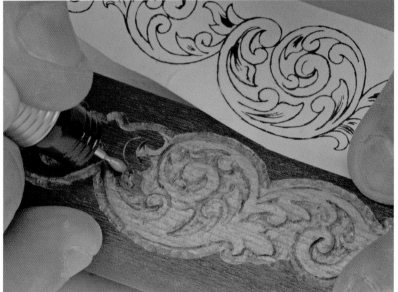

Use the pattern to create this leaf. Push in as you go. Smooth out the top a little bit.

The leaf is complete. Smooth out the top a little. Moving on the round off the sides of the next scroll. The rest of the carving is a repetition of what we have done before.

On this leaf we are going a bit deeper.

Finishing up the final scroll.

The completed carving so far.

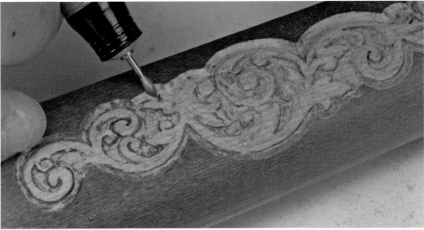

Now we will do two things at once, clearing the background and smoothing the outer edge of the scroll. Smoothing in progress.

Follow the contours around the outer edge, continuing to smooth the background and clean up the outer edge.

The outline is smoother now and about 1/8" in diameter.

Change to a small diamond football for smoothing the rest of the lines out, touching up small imperfections. The inner edge of this scroll line was not sharply defined, so I'm going back to smooth it further.

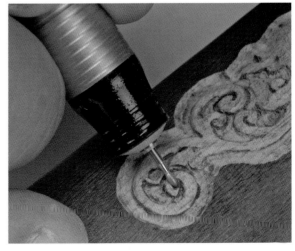

Now scoop the rest of the insides of the tendrils.

Making the starting tendril a bit deeper.

Here's the level of detail you can create with the small football.

Separating the leaf here so it can be part of the other scroll.

Separating this line a little more, allowing it to run underneath a bit.

Here on the main scroll I like to push the football in at an angle to create a deep impression and then round off the top edges created.

Go back to the small tendrils and make sure they all have small, scooped centers, as they should.

Separating the leaves from the tendrils now.

Look around to see what else needs to be done. I like to cut a small indent into the top of this leaf.

Now that the carving is done, touch it up a little with the 220 grit sandpaper stick. Go lightly over the carving, but make sure not to touch the rest of the stock you aren't working with. Use the sanding sticks if you are uncomfortable working with regular sandpaper in such small areas.

The carving is complete and sanded, now we will start stippling with a #2 carbide.

Move the bit up and down in the negative space areas to create little dots. Use a random pattern to do the stippling.

Be very careful not to hit the sides of the scrolls. All of this is done in a random pattern. This is also a chance to clean up small areas you couldn't before with the larger bits. The smaller the bit (a #4, #2, or #1 may be used), the nicer the look but the longer it will take to complete the stippling process.

Now stipple into the outside edge, moving from inner edge to outer in a random order.

Looking back, I see this section of scrolling appears too thick, so I use the #2 bit to make a small separation line in the middle of the scroll.

The stippling is complete and this scrollwork is done.

Lightly go over the carving with a sanding stick to remove any sharp edges. As you are sanding, run your fingers over the scrollwork to see if any sharp edges remain. If not, remove loose saw dust with a nylon brush.

The first project is done. We will stain this piece later, after we have finished the stock itself.

We are ready to begin the next project. Here are the patterns and the Mylar paper.

Our first job will be to position the wildlife and scrolls on the butt stock. Square up the pattern with the back of the stock, measuring with a card or a ruler, whichever you prefer. I like the card because sometimes with the ruler I can forget the measurement as I'm checking positioning and that never happens with the mark on my card.

We will start on the deer. The scrollwork will be a repetition of what we have done before. Once the pattern is down, use a #7611 carbide bit at a 90-degree angle to outline the pattern.

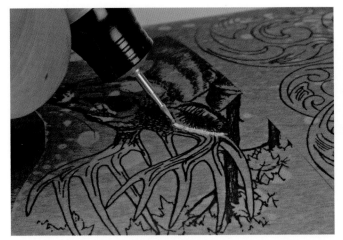

I'm starting with very light cuts along the top edge of the ear, showing me where the ear and antlers will be. These cuts are just barely going beyond the Mylar.

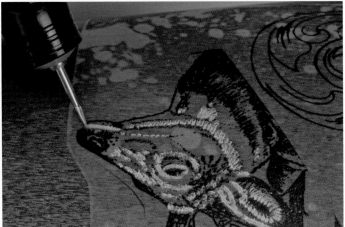

Outline the rest of the ear and now outline the major muscle groups, starting with the jaw line. Gently outline the eye. Next outline where the brow is going to be. Outline underneath the eye as well. Continue outlining.

Separate the mouth from the nose with a very thin line.

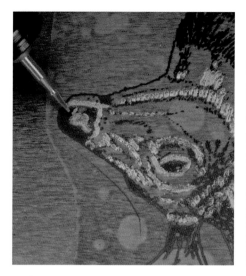

Define the nostril area. And now we can start cutting.

The initial outline cut outside of the line is about 1/16" deep.

I've decided to join the deep pattern to the scroll. Extend the neckline.

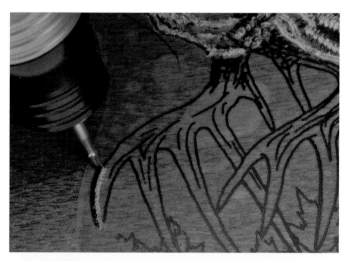

Be very careful when carving the antlers. This is where newcomers to the field often make mistakes. They cut the antlers too narrow. Keep to the very outside of the lines. Cut them fatter and we can always take away more later as needed.

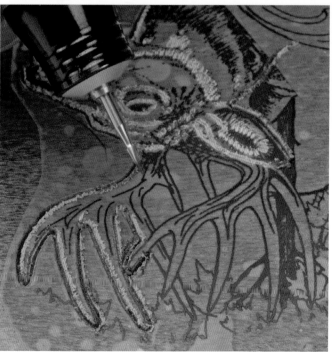

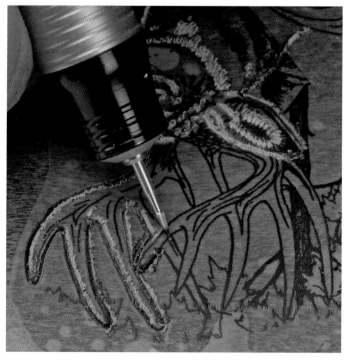

This is tricky where the antlers overlap. First cut away from the overlap, then cut around the antler that crosses over and finally make a thin crosshatch over the intersection very lightly.

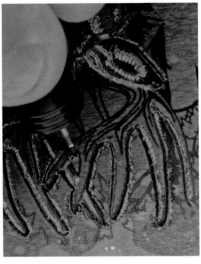

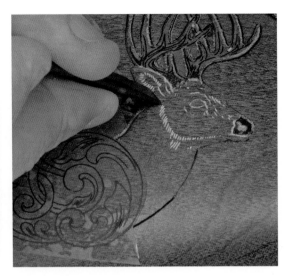

This small triangle between antlers is very tricky. Carve at an angle along the outside edge of the antler pattern.

Now remove the stencil as before.

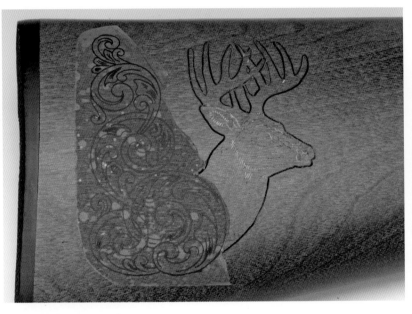

Here's the deer so far.

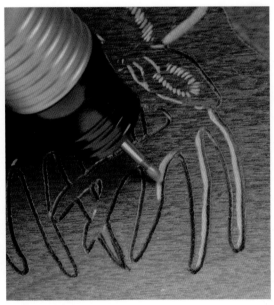

Take a small football bit and start outlining the deer. At a 45-degree angle, start outlining the antlers.

Turn the project around to start carving the other side of the antlers.

Now very lightly start removing the rest of the wood from the top of the antlers.

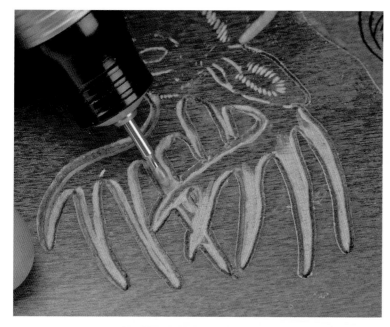

Be very careful to cut a little deeper here so the antler below is recessed beneath the antler above.

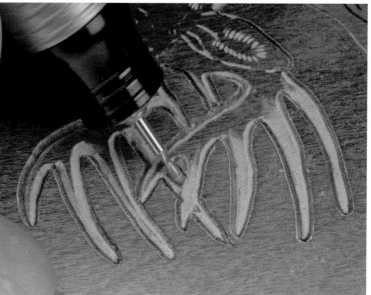

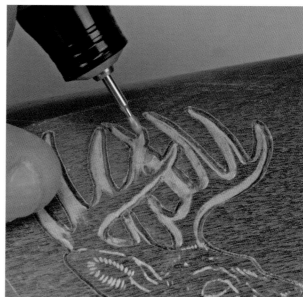

Make sure to go deeper in this small section as well, remembering to rotate the carving to get both sides of that section of antler.

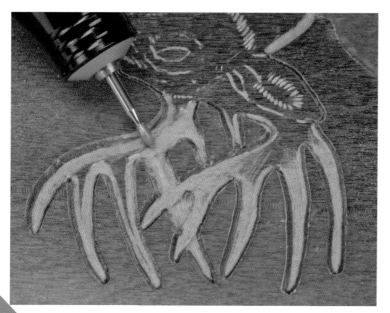

Even though it has been cut a little deeper, you still need to cut the edges of the antler below at a 45-degree angle to round it. Removing excess wood from the antler, remembering to cut a little deeper as this antler is in the background and the other is in the foreground.

Separating this antler from the back of the ear.

Separating the head from the antlers with small, sharp strokes.

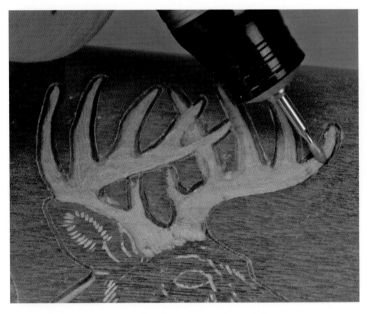

Continuing to recess the back antler to show it is further back.

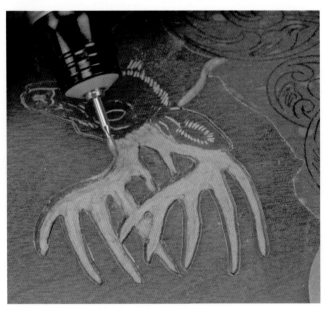

Create a small notch where the antler tines meet.

Outlining the shape of the head at a 45-degree angle.

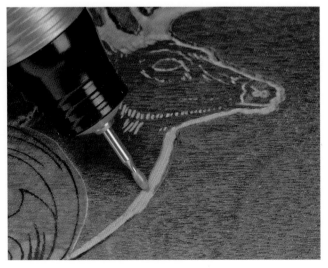

Continue working down the neck.

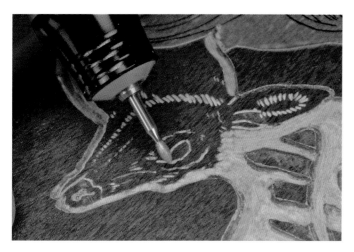
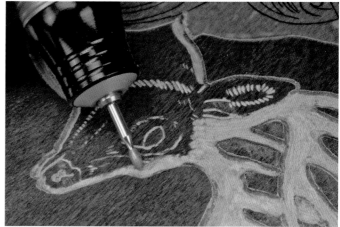

Flatten this area a bit above the other eye and then barely touch the area of the eye socket for the opposite eye.

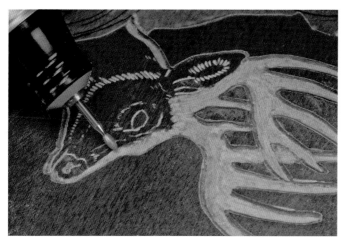

Flatten the area of the forehead and the area below the opposite eye as well.

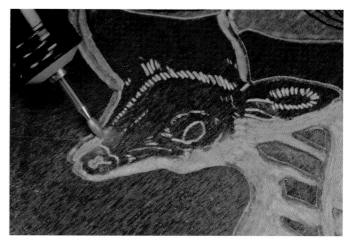

To define the area of the mouth, cut a very fine line along the line of the mouth and then gently lower the lower jaw area beneath the mouth.

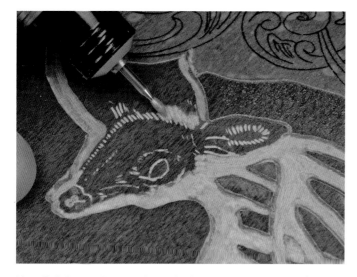

Very lightly cut deeper along the jaw line, using vertical strokes once again.

Extend a little behind the ear as well.

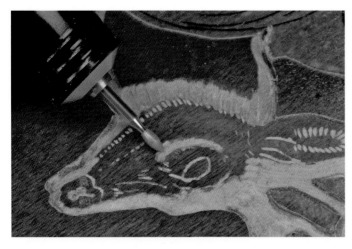

Make a very small indentation beneath the eye socket as well.

Change to a #171 carbide bit, and use this to redefine the inside of the ear at a 45-degree angle.

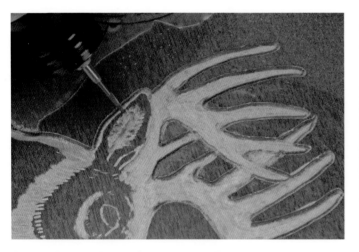

Carving in the middle of the ear as well.

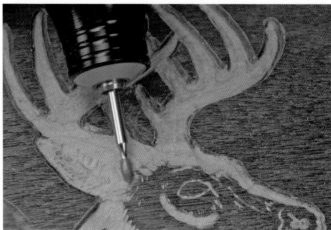

Change back to a small football and very lightly go over the edges of the ear. The grain is all smoothed away from the ear and the shaping of the ear is done.

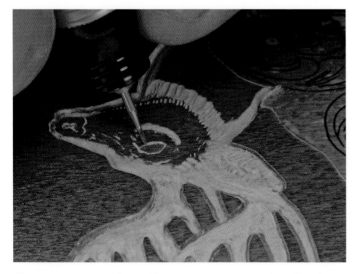

Change to a #901 bit, making sure to use a seating die when seating it or you will break the sharp point. Use this to very lightly follow the outline of the eye.

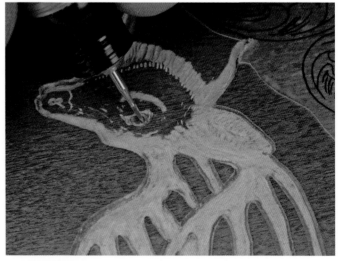

Remember to put the tear duct canal on the eye. The center of the eye is taking shape. The next part is tricky. Use the shoulder of the bit to round off the eye all around.

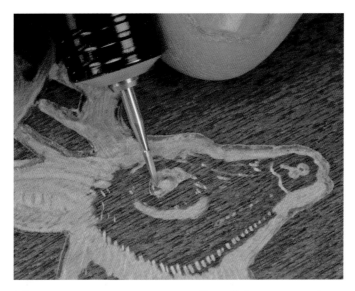

You will make several passes rounding off the eye, each time rounding off a little more. Rounding the eye. This is the most important feature. If the rest of the head is nice, but the eye is wrong, the whole image will not work.

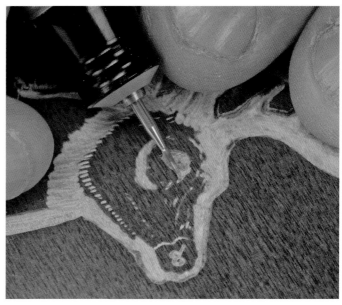

The eye has been rounded. Deepening the corners of the eyes just a little bit.

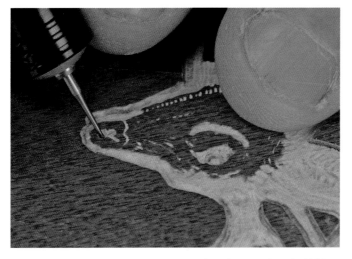

Change to a .5 carbide bit and a seating dye to place it. With this small bit we will form the nostril cavities. Cut in deep in the nostril.

Switch to a large football and keep on working to remove the rest of the wood lightly from the remaining portions of the deer.

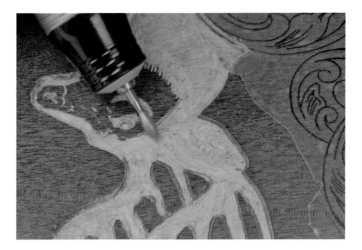

I'm shaping the back and lowering it below the area of the scrollwork.

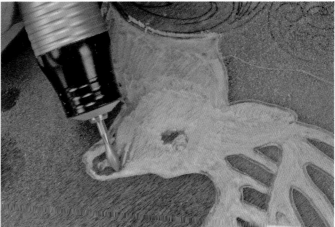

In the area of the face, just barely remove the surface of the wood.

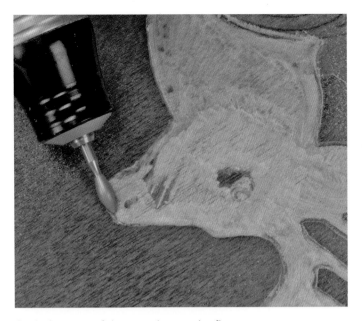

Sculpting part of the nose here to be flat.

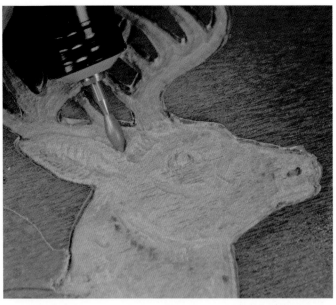

Carve a little deeper into the indentations to show the bone structure, particularly along the back of the jaw. Carve in the bony tissue where the antlers meet the head.

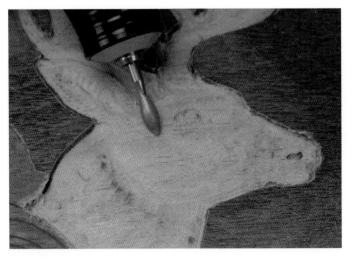

Even up this area, giving it more contour.

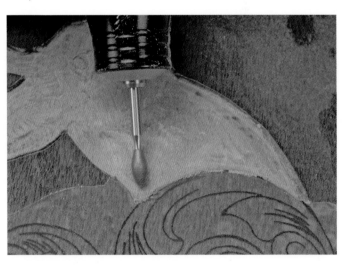

Carve in deeply along the scrolls to give the impression the deer is coming out from behind the scrolls.

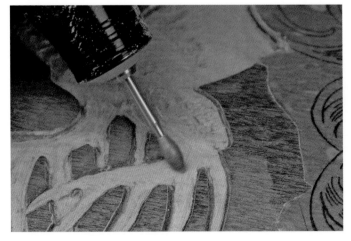

Moving on to the antlers, make sure to move the bit in the direction of the antlers, from the base outward, to show the direction of the antler growth.

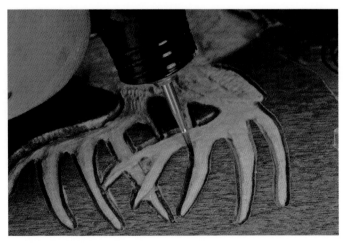

Switch to a #7611 bit and go over the outline to separate the antlers from the regular stock of the wood.

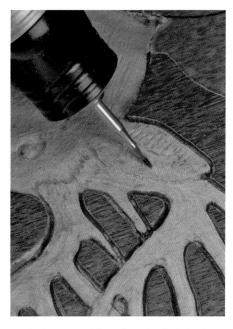

With the same bit, refine the hair in the ear area.

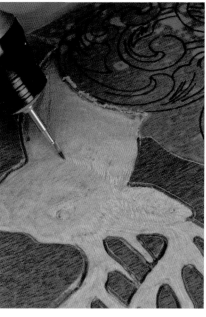

Carve in hair along the back and along the edge of the jawbone using a random pattern.

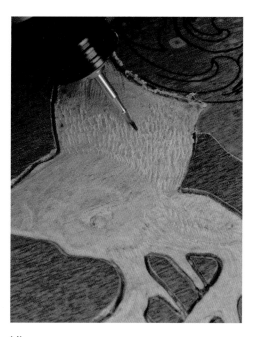

Like so.

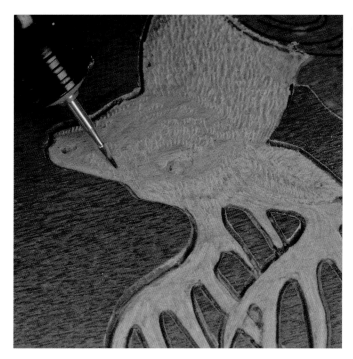

Carving in the facial features.

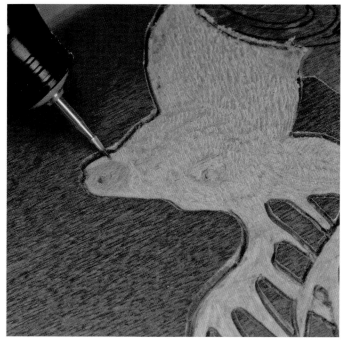

Try not to place any hair on the nose as this area is cartilage and hairless.

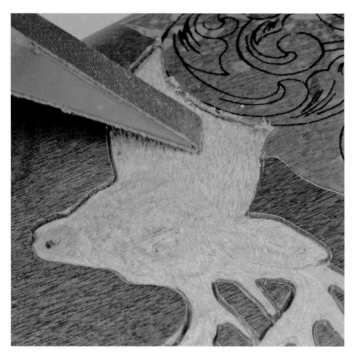

Use a 240 grit sanding stick to remove the rough edges.

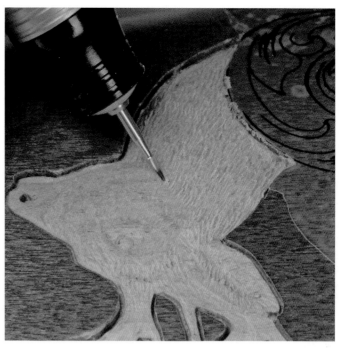

After the light sanding, touch up the hair a bit.

Brush off excess sawdust with a nylon brush and the deer if finished. It is time to move on to the scrollwork. Refer to the previous project for instruction on completing the scrollwork.

Carving the scrollwork on the pistol grip area of the stock with the whitetail deer carving. We're going to approach the scrollwork a little differently in this area. Use the #7611 bit to scratch the location to separate the tendrils from the leaves. This gives you an idea of where the outlines are.

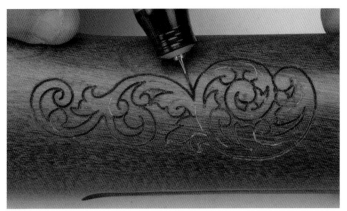

Switch to a #699 bit and proceed in carving the scroll as before. Remember, you want to carve to the outside of the scroll lines; otherwise the lines will look too skinny. The pattern is outlined along the outside of the scroll lines again and the Mylar has been removed as before. Notice that once the pattern has been removed, you can clearly see the small guide lines that were produced with the #7611 bit, clearly showing the separation points between the leaves and the scrolls.

Use the #6 bit to separate the wood from the artwork.

Using a large football, round off the edges and scrolls.

Once the edges are rounded, use the sandpaper stick to knock off the sharp edges. Use the #2 bit for the stippling, as before.

The last thing to do is sign your work. Use a #901 bit for this. Make sure to use the seating die to attach this fine bit.

THE STAINING PROCESS

Begin the staining process by applying pre-stain wood conditioner to the project. Once the pre-stain has dried, apply a second coat.

Now it is time to stain the deer and scroll on the stock and the associated forearm. Using a very fine brush I start by staining the negative space. This is Ebony stain for maximum contrast.

The Ebony stain has been applied to the background. Because the wood soaks up a lot of stain, even after applying several coats of pre-stain, you may want to use a second coat.

We now have the Ebony background stain on the stock and forearm and are ready to stain the deer.

Stain the deer with Special Walnut. We deal with the antlers separately as they require a light touch. I use two coats on the deer and one coat on the antlers, leaving the antler tips untouched.

 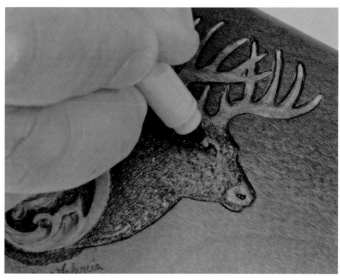

Use a paper towel or soft cloth to remove much of the stain applied to the antlers so that they can stay on the lighter side. Also use your cloth to clean off any excess stain.

I use a Sharpie to blacken in the center of the eye.

The deer is complete.

We are using a combination of TruOil and Mineral Spirits to seal and protect the carvings. I use a 50-50 mix. Apply with a paintbrush.

SHOTGUN CARVING BASKET WEAVE AND *LEAVES*

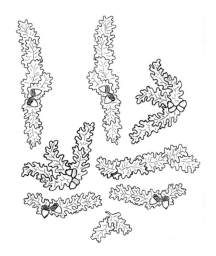

Full-size Patterns may be found on pgs. 53 & 55

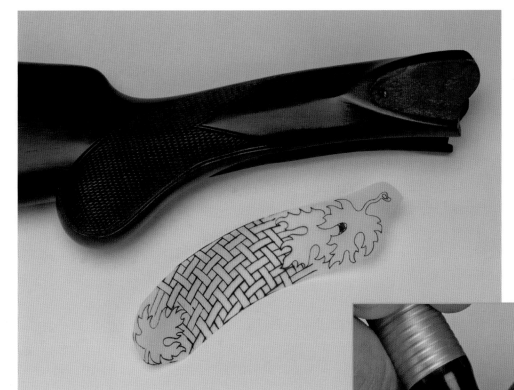

On the Huglu CZ-USA 28 gauge double barrel shotgun stock, we will replace the factory checkering with basket weave and maple leaves. Place the patterns as before. The pattern is fashioned to the area where we want it to fit; however, we will need to remove the factory checkering before we can do so. As you can see here, the stock has been removed from all of the hardware for ease of manipulating. If you are carving for a client, make sure you keep all the small screws and equipment in a container or, preferably, have the client give you the stock by itself.

Remove the checkering with a large football, beginning along the inside. Stay inside the second cut line on your first pass.

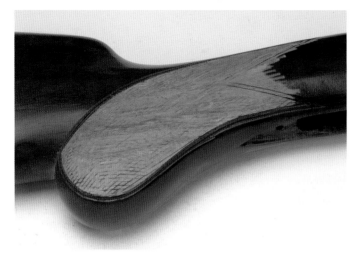

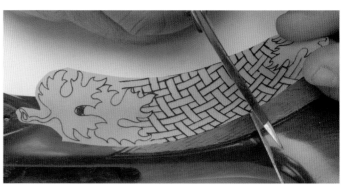

Make several small cuts along the edges of the pattern so it will lie flat when applied to the curved surface of the stock.

Enough of the checkering has now been removed to work with.

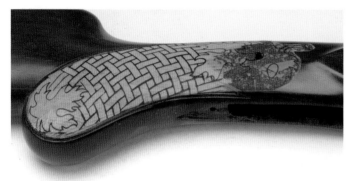

Remove the backing and carefully apply the Mylar pattern to the stock.

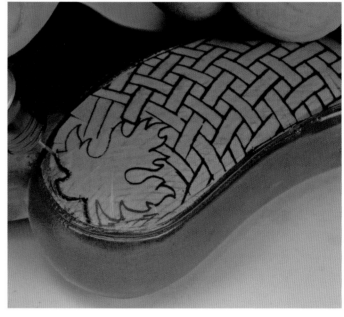

Use a #699 carbide bit and begin cutting the leaf pattern outlines. Cut the leaf patterns at a 90-degree angle.

The top leaves overlap. When working along the pattern line where the leaves overlap, do not cut too deep. There is one place here, where the drill bit is resting, that will be negative space and cut deeper than either of the leaves.

For this outlining I'm only cutting about 1/16" deep.

The underlying leaf has had the outline cut, and I'm moving on to the overlying leaf now.

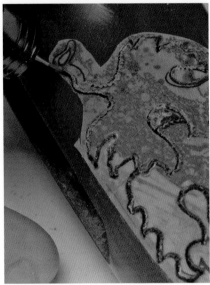

The stem is an area where you need to be very concerned. Make sure to cut along the very outer edge of the stem in order not to cut it too thin.

The basket weave is another area of concern. The small square will be taken down deep while the overlapping lines will not. So, cut lightly on the overlaps and deeply within the squares. Stop after cutting along the line of the square and do not cut the overlapping portion of the weave pattern. Cut deeply into the next square and lightly in the underlying portion of the weave. Repeat this process until the basket weave is outlined. Make sure to stay to the outside of the lines or your basket weave will be very thin.

Once the basket weave pattern lines running one direction have been cut, working from top to bottom, begin cutting the lines running the other direction, once again starting at the top. There is no easy way to do this.

As you begin cutting the second set of basket weave lines, you will note the squares are becoming quite prominent.

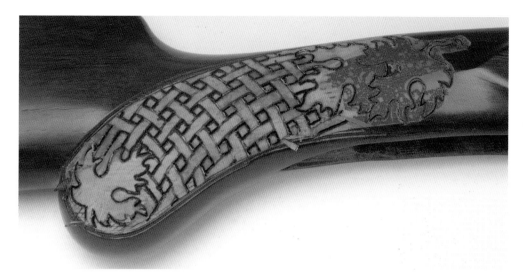

The pattern is now completely outlined and it is time to remove the stencil.

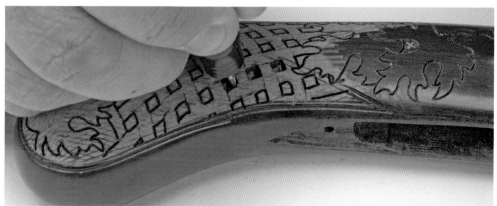

Use bit #703 to remove excess wood from the negative space between the weaves. Work with this bit at a 90-degree angle. We're cutting about 1/8" deep and removing as much material as possible, but stay away from the corners for now. We will clean them up later.

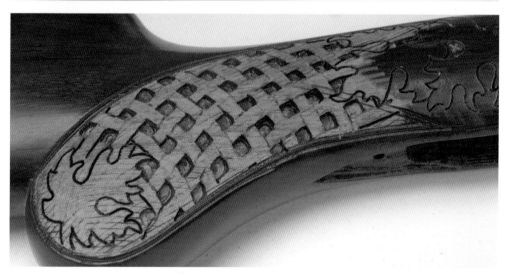

All of the squares of negative space have been removed.

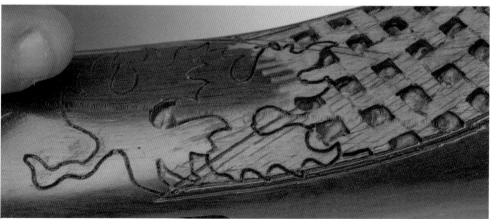

Using the same bit remove the negative space between the leaves out to a 1/8" depth as well.

Removing excess wood from around the outer edges of the leaves. This defines the leaves around the edge of the basket weave patterning.

Repeat this process around the leaf at the base of the stock as well. This angle gets a little awkward along the very base of the stock and leaf.

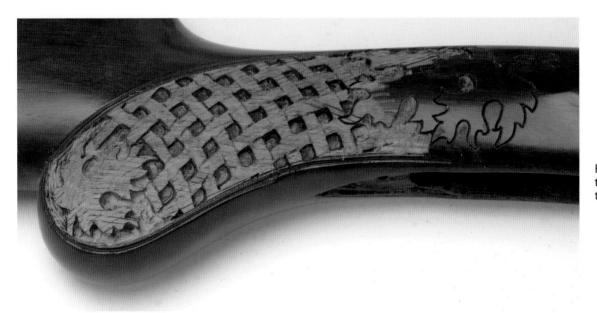

Progress. Now it is time to move on to the basket weave.

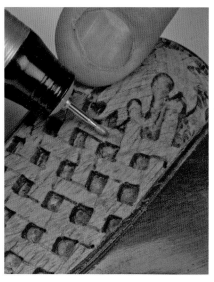

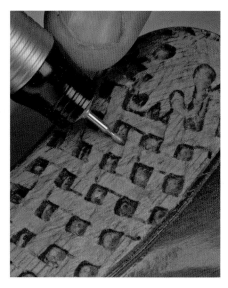

Change to a small football to carve the basket weave. I like to start along one line and move my way across, deepening the lines at the end that is away from the rise of the weave over the other weave.

Cut deep along the line of the weave that goes beneath the overlying weave line. Cut about half way down when the lines meet and slowly rise up as it approaches the overlapping point.

Once you finish one row, move one row down and over and start again.

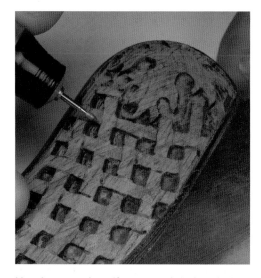

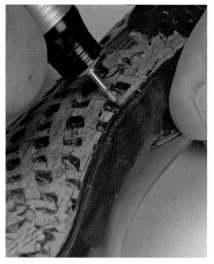

Here's a warning: If you are right handed, you will tend to cut deeper along the right hand edge and vice versa if you are left handed. Be very careful to avoid this tendency and keep your cuts even all the way across.

When you have finished one side, turn the stock upside down and start again, cutting deep where the weave goes under and rising up to the overlying weave. Work your way across row by row.

Once you've finished the line of weave that runs from the top of the stock to the bottom, rotate the stock and begin working on the weave that runs along the stock's length. Once again, work from left to right, top to bottom so you keep your place. It would be very easy to get the weave pattern mixed up and ruin the effect.

This one along the very edge is tricky. You only want to go a little deep, barely touching this as it is on the outer edge.

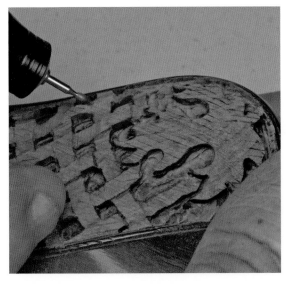

Turn the stock one last time to follow the last line of weave from left to right and top to bottom. That is the base of the stock handgrip on the right.

The basket weave pattern is now complete.

Switch to a #171 bit and clean up the negative space, squaring the corners as you go. Some of the corners were rounded during the carving. Sharpen and square them up. The lines should all be crisp.

The basket weave is complete. Now it is time to add texture with the same bit at a 45-degree angle on the weave. Very lightly touch the surface to add texture.

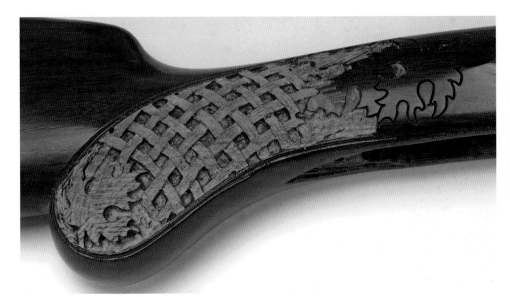

Once you've finished texturing the weave in one direction, turn the stock around and begin texturing in the other direction. During the texturing process you find out if you carved the weave properly all the way across. The reeds of the basket weave are now finished. It is time to move on to the leaves.

Switch to a large football bit and start working on the underlying leaf, separating it from the overlying leaf.

Make the area in the middle of the underlying leaf more concave.

Be more aggressive cutting away wood in the center of the leaf when it is overlapped by the top leaf.

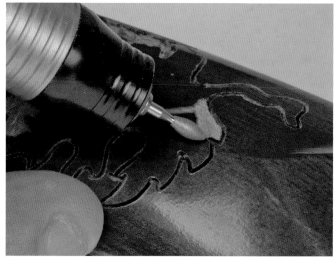

Moving on to the overlying leaf, be careful as you work around the edge that you don't extend outside the line into the stock.

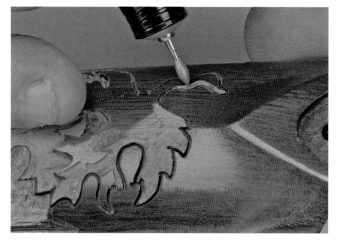

Pay particular attention when cutting the stem, rounding it off at a 45-degree angle but not making it too thin. Just lightly round off that area.

Lightly carve the top and then get more aggressive in the middle of the leaf, adding pattern and depth.

 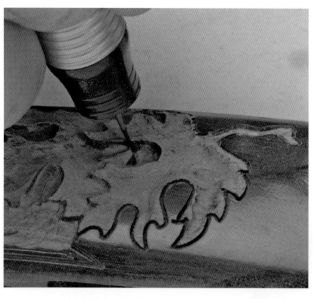

Continue contouring and shaping the leaf. Use a #703 bit to clean out the area of negative space between the leaves.

Switch to a #699 to get the small edges you couldn't reach with the #703.

Return to the large football bit and carve the last leaf. Along this side, I'm toning down the edges to the leaf so they will not catch on anyone's clothes. Take off the sharp edges from the other leaves as well.

Switch to a #8 diamond bit and slow down the drill from 40 psi to 20 psi. At this speed, use the #8 diamond to smooth the leaves out and soften them.

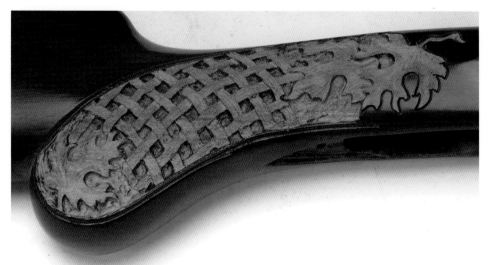

The leaves are softened up now. Return the regulator pressure to 40 psi.

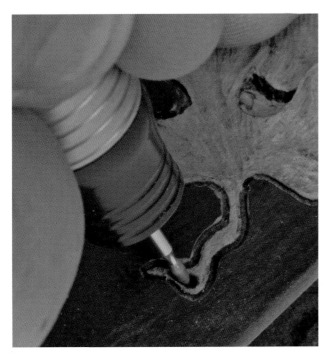 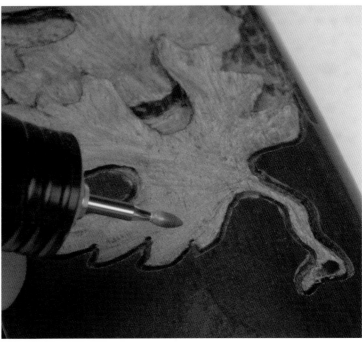

Use a small football to create a finishing touch. Push it in deep in the end of the leaf stem and pull it gently up at an angle to create the end of the leaf stem.

Use a #2 carbide to add stippling to all of the negative space. When stippling the little squares, use a pattern, left to right, top to bottom. That way you won't forget any of the squares.

This carving is complete.

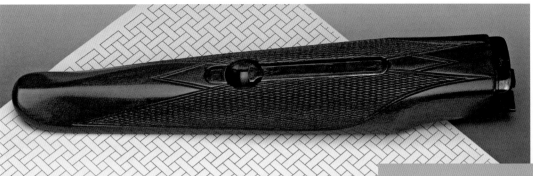

Here is the basket weave pattern we will use on the forearm.

We are working with the forearm of the shotgun now. I traced the outline of the checkering on a piece of onion paper so I can cut the appropriate size of the Mylar.

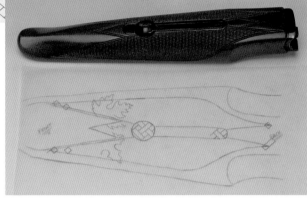

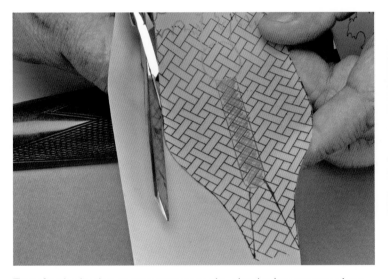

Transfer the basket weave pattern to the checkering pattern piece, apply it to Mylar, and cut out the Mylar pattern.

Now cut each half of the pattern individually so it may be properly applied to the forearm.

At this point we need to remove the checkering as before and follow the instructions above for adding the basket weave pattern, leaves, and stippling.

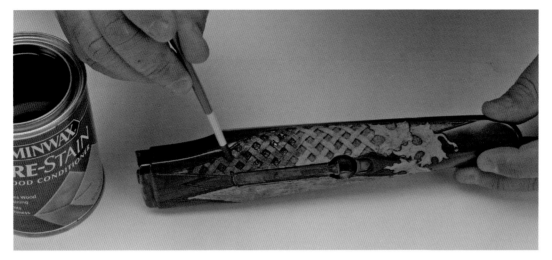

Begin the staining process by applying pre-stain wood conditioner to the project. Once the pre-stain has dried, apply a second coat. After the second coat dries, you can now apply the stain as described in the previous project.

The Ebony background stain has been applied to the stock and forearm.

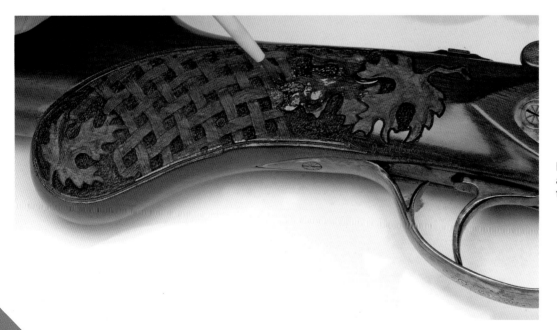

Repeating the staining and sealing process on the basket weave pattern.

PATTERNS

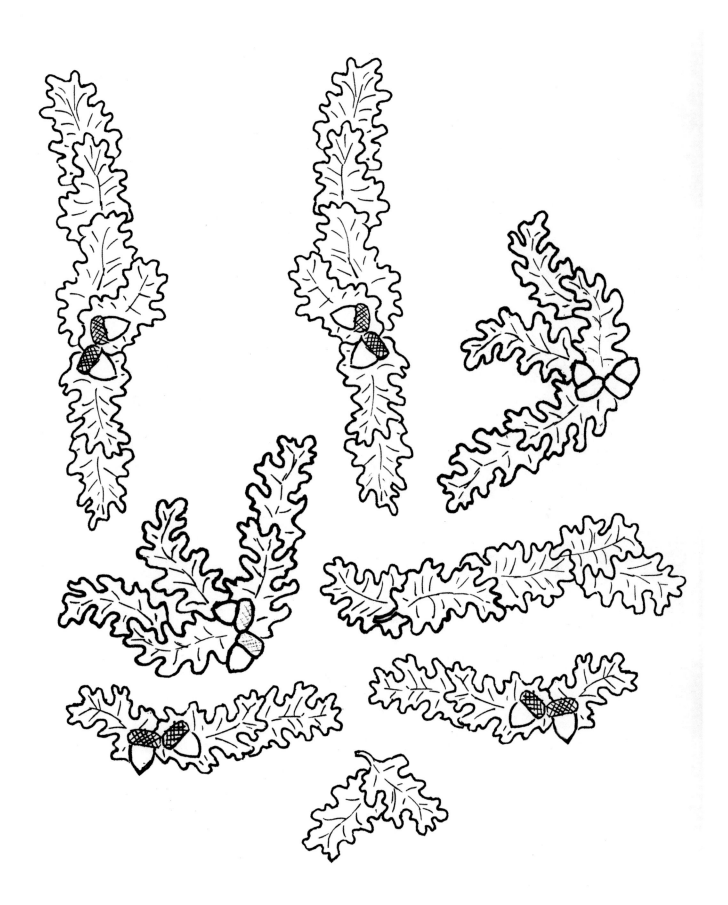

Note: Basketweave Pattern is shown 50% 0f original size. For a full-size pattern, enlarge 200%.

Gunstock Carving:

GALLERY

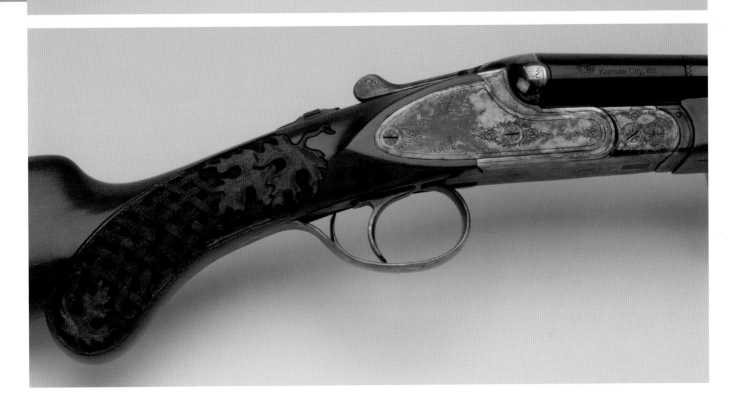

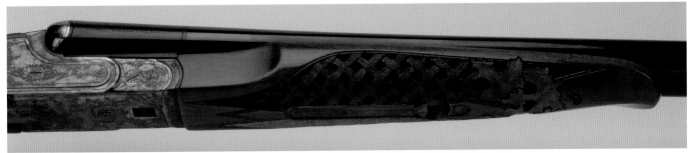

Photo © Jose Valencia.

Photo © Jose Valencia.

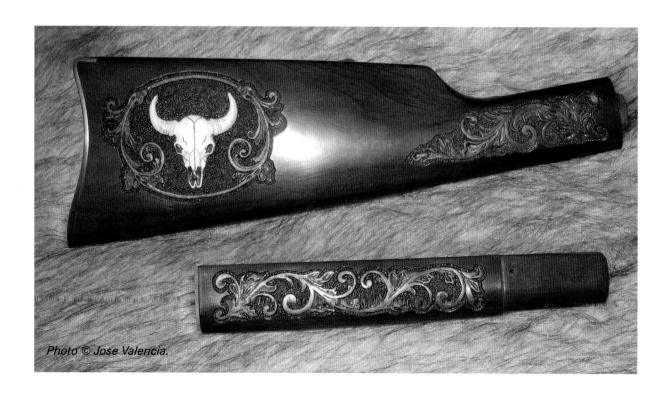

Photo © Jose Valencia.

Photo © Jose Valencia.

Photo © Jose Valencia.

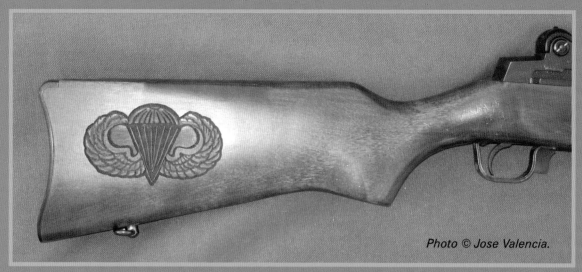

Photo © Jose Valencia.

Photo © Jose Valencia.

Photo © Jose Valencia.

Photo © Jose Valencia.

Photo © Jose Valencia.

Photo © Jose Valencia.

Photo © Jose Valencia.

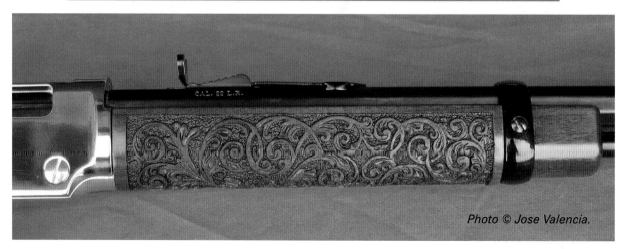

Photo © Jose Valencia.

Photo © Jose Valencia.

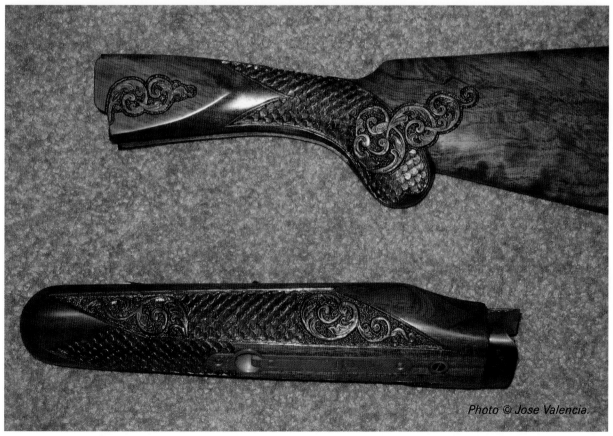

Photo © Jose Valencia.

GUNSTOCK CARVING CLASSES

By Jose Valencia

USING THE POWER PEN

I have classes available where you can come and learn to carve using the High Speed Power Pen.

My studio is located at the base of South Mountain in Phoenix, Arizona.

You will receive personal attention as our classes are four students maximum.

Classes are available on the following:

Carving leaves.
Carving feathers.
Basket weave pattern.
Fish scale pattern.
Carving scrolls.
Carving wildlife.
Turquoise inlays.
Cast ivory inlays.

We have two and three day classes available, depending on the subjects you would like to learn. Please call my studio for details at 480-415-4245.

I provide all supplies for the class, snacks, beverages, and lunch.

If you already have a high speed drill, please bring it with you, along with your burs.

If you do not have one, I can provide one for you free of charge.

I can also show you how to get your own Power Pen at a discount.

Check my website www.guncarving.com for a class schedule.

To reserve a seat in a class, please call me at 480-415-4245 or e-mail me at jose@ josevalenciastudio.com

If you would like a different date for a class, I also offer customized wood carving classes upon request.

If you do not know if high speed carving is for you, and you do not want to spend the money on the high speed Power Pen and classes and then find out it is not for you…

…try the tool risk free!

I have a two hour class where you can try the Power Pen and do a couple of wood and glass projects to find out if this is the right tool for you.

WARNING: high speed carving is very addicting.